Markets Around the World

by Susan Ring

STECK-VAUGHN
Harcourt Supplemental Publishers

www.steck-vaughn.com

We all shop for things we need.
At a market, people can buy many different things.
This is a farmer's market in the United States.

Farmers grow fruits and vegetables. People come to farmer's markets to buy food fresh from the farm.

Where do pumpkins grow?

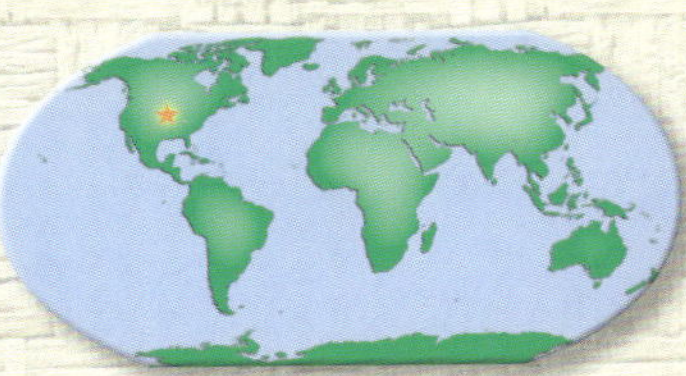

What does a map of the United States look like?

What kind of money is used in the United States?

There are different kinds of markets all around the world. This is a spice market in India.

Look at all the different spices!
People buy these spices to use in cooking.
The spices make food tasty.

Where does cinnamon come from?

What does a map of India look like?

What kind of money is used in India?

This is a camel market in Egypt.
People come here to buy and sell camels.

People use camels to help carry things. Camels can travel far in the hot desert without much water.

What does a camel store in its hump?

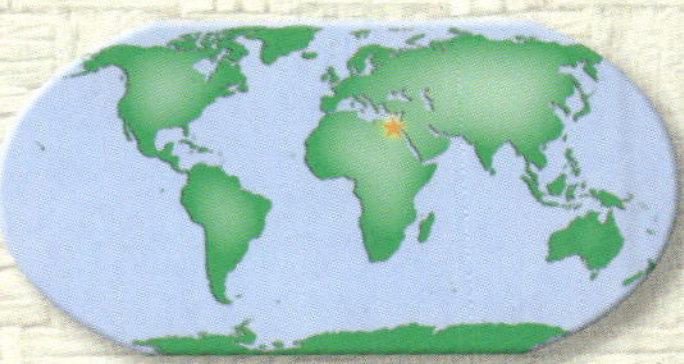

What does a map of Egypt look like?

What kind of money is used in Egypt?

This is a fabric market in Senegal.
Many kinds of colorful cloth are for sale.

People use the cloth to make clothing. They will sew the fabric into long, colorful robes.

What are the colorful robes called?

What does a map of Senegal look like?

What kind of money is used in Senegal?

Women are selling blankets at this outdoor market in Peru. The colorful blankets are covered with beautiful designs.

People make these blankets by hand. The blankets are made with yarn that is spun from wool.

What animal does the wool in Peru come from?

What does a map of Peru look like?

What kind of money is used in Peru?

Some markets are on the water.
This floating market is on a canal in Thailand.

Boats dock along a walkway. People in the boats sell all kinds of things to people along the sidewalk.

What are some of the things for sale at this market?

What does a map aof Thailand look like?

What kind of money is used in Thailand?

This is a fruit market in Jamaica.
Look at all of the delicious kinds of fruit for sale.

Nearby farmers grow these fruits.
Buyers try to make a deal with the sellers.
They both want to get the best price.

What fruit do people in Jamaica eat instead of potatoes?

What does a map of Jamaica look like?

What kind of money is used in Jamaica?

This is a pottery market in Mexico.
People can buy pots of all shapes and sizes at this market.

Many pots are stacked together.
Artists make each pot by hand.
The big pots take a long time to make.

What is used to make the pots?

What does a map of Mexico look like?

What kind of money is used in Mexico?

This is a fish market in Australia.
It is one of the largest fish markets in the world.

People come here to buy fresh fish. They can also buy other kinds of seafood, such as shrimp and crab.

What is the largest fish sold in the market?

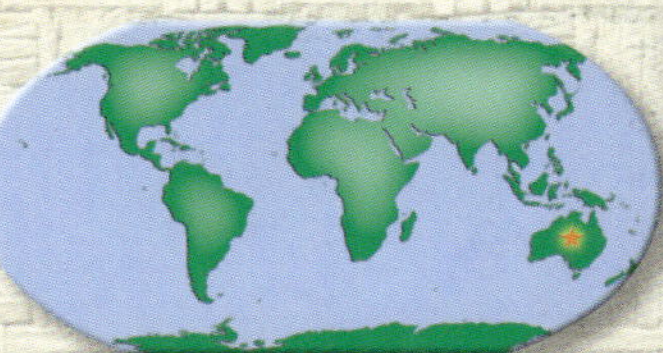

What does a map of Australia look like?

What kind of money is used in Australia?

This is a cheese market in the Netherlands. The only thing for sale at this market is cheese!

The cheese comes in large, round wheels. People who buy the cheese cut the wheels into smaller pieces.

How much does one wheel of cheese weigh?

What does a map of the Netherlands look like?

What kind of money is used in the Netherlands?

This is a rug market in Morocco.
Morocco is famous for its beautiful rugs.

It takes a long time to weave each rug. Different colors of wool are woven together to make bright patterns.

What kind of machine do people use to weave the rugs?

What does a map of Morocco look like?

What kind of money is used in Morocco?

There are markets all around the world.
Some markets are on land.
Others are on the water.
Some markets sell food.
Others sell things that people use.

What would you like to buy at a market?